VANITAS, ROUGH

ALSO BY LISA RUSS SPAAR

Satin Cash
Blue Venus
Glass Town

All That Mighty Heart: London Poems (editor)
Acquainted with the Night: Insomnia Poems (editor)

VANITAS, ROUGH

LISA RUSS SPAAR

P O E M S

A Karen & Michael Braziller Book

PERSEA BOOKS / NEW YORK

Persea Books, Inc.
277 Broadway
New York, NY 10007

Library of Congress Cataloging-in-Publication Data

Spaar, Lisa Russ.
Vanitas, rough : poems / Lisa Russ Spaar.—1st ed.
    p. cm.
"A Karen & Michael Braziller book."
Includes bibliographical references and index.
ISBN 978-0-89255-420-1 (original trade pbk. : alk. paper)
I. Title.
PS3568.U7644V36 2012
811'.54—dc23
                         2012026918
First edition
Printed in the United States of America
Designed by Rita Lascaro

CONTENTS

ACKNOWLEDGMENTS

Grateful acknowledgment is made to the editors of the following publications in which some of these poems first appeared, occasionally in a different version or with an alternative title.

32 Poems: "Bone Orchard Lunch Hour"
Alabama Literary Review: "Music Lessons"
Arts & Sciences Magazine: "Black Snake"
Blackbird: "St. Home" and "St. Bed of Snow"
Boston Review: "Hibernalphilia"
Cerise Press: "St. Saint"
The Collagist: "Graven"
Denver Quarterly: "Vanitas, Rough," "St. Protagonist," and "St. Volition"
The Kenyon Review: "Kismet"
Meridian: "Two Shrifts," "Thaw," and "The Middle Ages, Bonus Track"
Pembroke Magazine: "St. Vogue"
Poetry: "Departures: Chapter One" and "Midas Passional"
Ploughshares: "Goldfinches" and "Whether"
Plume: "Trouble"
Shenandoah: "*Cathartes aura*" and "After the Meeting, a Red Fox"
SLATE: "The Irises"
Southwest Review: "Hang Fire"
Spirituality & Health: "Trailing Mary & Martha: 3 AM"
Virginia Quarterly Review: "Old Rose" and "Christmas Stoup"
Women's Voices for Change: "God's Gym"

A debt of inestimable gratitude to the John Simon Guggenheim Foundation and Carole Weinstein for their support during the making of this book, and abiding thanks to Karen and Michael Braziller, and especially to my editor, Gabriel Fried.

VANITAS, ROUGH

St. Protagonist

It's bedtime. Tell me a story
as the leaves fly

again, even as we love them
& cannot see them.

Espouser, hero, night errant—
whose wont is to belaud,

chant, cheer, adore
what is before you:

teach me that. The part
in the lady's long dark hair.

The part where that does not matter.
And the ending, sobbed through,

where the improbable becomes
not true, but nonetheless believed.

Departures: Chapter One

Morning's mirage, disdainful & calm
    as a mirror,

held the shorn bush that yesterday
    flourished,

now lopped canes & a scant spitfall
    of remnance,

confetti trampled in the clefts
    of vanishing deer.

To touch its truth I punched my fist
    into the chopped molest,

the boscage—withdrew my red sleeve.
    Abstract that.

St. Saint

Even my dreams won't reveal you,
though the hand wants its scepter.

Instead, the sublimity of backdrop,
All Hallows, solemn close of paschal drawers,

wounded stare, the all-out decking of box stores.
Fa la la, la la. O beloved departed, la-la, la-la,

obligate me, after work, a long day in a body,
passing beneath blooded lintels, maples, red oaks—

interpreters, I might be so bold to call them—
to sing in sacrifice, from century to century.

Your tale is not mine, of course,
to tell. But the world is ingot-cast

cinders now & this hour already a beyond.
What weary head doesn't crave its nimbus?

St. Chardonnay

I have two throats—felted
    intervals.

Call me lonely. Anything
    you like.

No gold quite breaks the dusk
    to smithereens

like self-pity going down
    easy.

Lest this be merely
    a drunken poem,

let a mythic figure sidle in,
    cosmic,

marigolds in the mouth
    & magnificent.

Or worse, bring on her lesser
    coz, Empowerment. Ha.

Two throats & each a sacred force.
    But who would want

to talk about that.
    To talk at all.

Old Rose

Against black matchsticks,
        rotted fangs,
plus and minus, sum lines, mathematics,

the shear, the jabbing jaws
        in elbow-high gloves
& up to the briary cervix, a welter historical,

in situ, battling climbing *Old Blush*.
        Grief in this devastation,
this mess, grapevine, scarlet creeper, demolished nests.

Wasps in venomous rapture of ousting.
        Velvet foreskin,
underarms beaked with bite tugs,

romance and its fugue.
        And the nicknames? Abide in them,
free—*Constance Spry, Awakening, Alchemist.*

The year's turning? How ever pinpoint
        the first splinter fault in any fallen temple?
I turned for my love & only him.

Knowing this, to brave this subtracted cage;
        for him, the flail & scourge,
the hurt, the bled, the bereft bed.

Trouble

after Rilke

And so it took shape, & from what.
True, a voice wept for you
while singing, from the year just past.
From your crib.

Almost, you became used to it,
& the laws of blood transmitting
from thin skins of strong, troubled wrists.
Morning like a scab.

Wind wrests a fallen paper by the nape,
twists as if it held your name inside.
The eternal is not interrupted by this
even as you cup it in your fists.

Solo Moon

A given, inconstancy.
If only I were wired for that gypsy

restless affair, his *yes, yes*
not mine to possess.

True, he is my guest,
breast where the arrow's fletch

shapes itself around a little rue
mostly mine to mistake for truth,

that zilch dimension.
But is to long for something

the same as to believe
in its abiding? Please.

Beyond the maudlin marquee
the trees expose themselves to me.

Don't their emptied cabinets
suggest each storied orb must rise & set?

Midas Passional

No one has touched me for weeks,
yet in this drugged, gilt afternoon, late,

when nothing is safe, I'm paralyzed,
as though so wildly desired—passing solo through the garden's

cinnamon, marigolds, famished roses, where a matted shingle
of the swept-up human hair I begged from a local beauty shop

& spread out fruitlessly among the blooms & thorns
to keep away the deer might well be a satyr

passed out in the palace's candied gold—
that something regnant with a strange, god-like power

could not help but reach out from the umbral blue
to tap my white arm. It is a day to die,

the light autoerotic, theatrical, with an unbearable listing,
stalled in cusp, in leonine torpor. Is courage artifice?

As though to answer were within my means.
Or to even move my mouth.

Goldfinches

If never was the question. Even then.
That *when* feels closer now

might embarrass me before this window,
more mirror than I would like at this hour,

bathos of years ghosting face, throat,
my impatient turning off of the lamp.

Now I'm small again, and the world outside
mysterious, perfumed, & large.

Were I not to feel this, would now
be when? I watch the primal arousal:

day's lost fruit stoned by black hills,
the metafucked in the metaphysical, &c.

Then five duskal flames assign me
the barkless dark, the barren cherry.

Still Life with Hare & Knife

When the witnesses sent their children,
mother was skinning rabbits.
What else to do,
pamphlet extended,
but call for her? Salvation! Watchtower!

Hands like maple leaves turned,
around the corner she came,
knife hung loose.
Coral reef of souring crabapples,
blue sky vitals, the cool paste of the brochure

as she cursed
the quailing clot of grown-ups retreating
in church coats, spectacles, booklets clutched
like shields as they shoved their brood behind them,
backed away. She cursed them again

and again, sending the innocent to do
their dirty work. Long white feet,
the rabbits had
given off heat. On the picnic table,
they stiffened in a halo, gnats, mosquitoes

that bit me too, the rapture
transfused. What did it mean
to save or be saved
as acorns struck & webs appeared
overnight, child-sized, spangled, shrouded knots of dew?
Did it have to kill you?

Vanitas, Rough

In a panel of floor-propped mirror
your tongue in me is mine, too,

glass pear of the toppled goblet,
drunken wasp grazing semen yolk

of split, glazed oyster shells,
Death blowing soap bubbles

out the orbital sockets, glycerin
filming a halved walnut,

taut brains of meat a tinged pink
tulip petal falls toward

just as I rear up into stomp
of opened drawer, a third, raptor's eye,

blue-ish, topaz egg, already rising
in the drenched, heaving wilderness of our face.

Mono no aware

Flakes of snow blister the abandoned cup of wine
as by umbral coals a man, as he repeatedly enters,

also slowly draws from inside her one then another
fat, fresh-water, threaded pearl. Four feet flat

to a straw mat, sashes, robes, knees—curtains parted—
smother beneath which the stilted, polygamous house

is arrested, even the sweetfish and icicle heron a dream
in a forearm's thick, arrested glaze.

Yet no ice apart from water, as that which streams
from her eyes attests. There is pursuit, and there is pain.

Delicious from the dark he pulls from her what she insists:
scarlet knuckle of the bridge. Wisteria, twisted winter wrists.

Their souls, cypress, roasted tea, carp,
cast on shôji, abalone film, shucked and welded, apart.

Debt

This stable dawn, unplated,
shows me the world without me,

a different predicament from jealousy—
three players, one bed.

Your heart speaks of it in dactyls—
even the waters will close one day—

despite the pelvic altar, our share
of rented air, stairless landing

hiving our hair, like these trees, louche
with taboo green that lingers despite

the blooded syntax of exit.
Which even death cannot prove.

Broke

Inoperative, this ethanol pinch—
shives of magnolia-shed sleet

shekelling shoulders, toted books, scalp
this Candlemas, feast of the presentation,

blessing of the plummeting indicator,
lost retirement fund, accounting, the holy tallow;

feast of the gathering, the boreal
ice-storm into one's arms.

As at the glacial lintel of a cave, one sees
that certain futures cannot be distinguished:

the woman flush with ecstasy,
the woman penniless & drowning.

Kafka equated love
with a martyr's death. Lost anyway, day

vouches for night's barrow,
insolvent warrant of tomorrow.

Christmas Stoup

Ink slurs into byssal threads,
   split blue caskets of mussels
scapular in ritual archipelago, butter, cream,

the chowder pot a holy trencher
   on a night stour, bitter
with advent, wilted cruxes, tarragon,

bassinet of clamshell, shucked,
   fragile saddlebags,
houses primeval: slughead, mantle,

foot, all vulnerable, indomitable.
   Frozen tongues lengthen magnetically
at the cornices. The moon. Ah, the moon,

a cameo unspendable, the world
   in verbless fugue state, triad of thyme,
bay; the sorrowful sea by the body unlocked.

Blue Moon

Drop a coin into the poor box
of the dead doe stalling the road's portal.

Way out, yule cog, sear as bone, turn night
into day, the dream my old father told,

decanting hoar sod, beguiling winter
by shovelfuls & singing

despite the mustard seed of his waking,
his wife's forgetting an albino naught

all its own, endless amnesiac clearing,
endless sift, drift. The dead owl

of it swings, splayed, nailed
to a warning gate; dark has its way.

A candle socket weeps wax.
Keep the dying year as ye might,

yet here's time's seeping jaw;
woe's iris, looking on.

Without exultation, we're all dead
before its uppercut can do us wrong.

From a Life Under Jupiter

He entered conversations
morningless as dungeons.
All the old entrances in the woods
refused their extent.

To himself he felt a local affliction.
Crawl, said black heart, crow in a bare tree,
Crawl. Crawl. He did.
The sadness again of being again a son.

Night exaggerated nothing,
heavy tableware silvering
& no sign of the master or his bride.
Yet sadness dwelled far off,

celestial blister, & never wished
for him. The lonely bliss of going
where the body cannot follow.
Of knowing the foreign heap you are.

Trailing Mary & Martha: 3 AM

Difference—had begun—
  —Emily Dickinson

Outside, unfathomable barking.
Within, I'm quandary, a drupe

stapled by bees, a sink full of mastic plates.
An erotic scenario? The truth is

a prayer once saw you inside me;
how dare your absence now adjure

that fastening? That dog again.
Behind glass, trucks in gear-lust

jaw dumpsters in the cul-de-sacs
& I consider Dickinson in the sink room,

limestone chink of dinner dishes,
forks tuned against an enameled basin,

noon fracturing the room.
That figure in the doorway—

why not travel with him now?
The God-gene, of course;

expensive to know for whom we minister,
for whom we wake & sing.

Darning

Ledger of his wandering, these frayed harps
at heel and sole, & her running stitch through them,

eke basting, sumac in scarlet filet lace,
cider groves of oak through which the deer

skittish tuck & flow, needle dreaming what his body
carries, swelling in warp, now weft, that screed.

story of the saints, that we must wear ourselves
away to be filled, each suture a way: her delving

into his going, new maps thistling the talus wings
by which he always reappears.

St. Volition

Objects withstand the gaze
better than words.

This rush of leaves, for instance,
in copper light: how they persuade

with the squandering love can make
of days, ample spilling fistfuls.

I could look closely at *removed.*
But who would choose to return

that stare? Something beautiful
in the unusual arrangements

at the Corner lot. I try to park my car.
An argument of ice-felled limbs

obscures the painted spaces.
Clink. Laughter, voices coupled on a hot-house porch.

Sometimes I begin a train of thought
I am unwilling to pursue.

Whether

Maybe your baby done made some other plans.
　　—Stevie Wonder

Out of a kit of bones, the dog's half-cast
opiate eyes ask *can't you hear the moths, pelting*

the pear glass? & then there is nothing else I can hear.
Bulbs opal and ignited as felted anus-stars,

snow, spot the porch, blast the poplars:
the thumbscrew aortal pulse of Philomela.

Whose fork is this? my mother asked me, pointing to her cane
in the dark of the backseat last week. I was driving.

Probably one of the kids' I replied, *they're always trashing
my car,* but truly they are the brilliant canto of my antiquity.

I search her eyes, terrified, for signs of pain.
She is light, and waits not for the flip of a switch.

Nor is my love portable, quick lick in the discourse of the world.
For her, do I get down. For her, my fork and cane.

Billet-doux

Was I tired of being human
    when I dreamed that stub cicada,
blown cavity, bezeled mêlée of oblivion, blizzarding bees,

my wrists a slurry, melting snow
    contused with apple sap? I know hell
is freezing over, but still, the *seasons*—.

Winter is of course a mistake.
    Yet how else justify this indented nest,
daub & cowlick, frankly pubic, a fluster in the cold brake?

Even now—blue oval stones pecked from inside
    & long ago turned to angel wing, to wind—
I know I must not touch, lest I do them harm.

Thaw

Why does this sepia-whetted
lilac smoke extruding

with heartbroken restraint
between scrap oaks make me believe

in my own death as I have not,
even in that dusked moment,

a child on Key Pond,
when the toothed toe of my skate

halted, stunned above the fat-purled
floe of deer carcass, carmine bloom

bumping gently beneath the granular
blue icemelt, vinegar in my mouth,

plight that wed me to,
that showed me my *inside*?

Where will that go, I wonder?
Flocked foreskins of the tulip poplar

grow beyond this darkening hour.
Why would they not?

The Middle Ages, Bonus Track

Injurious, this color of birth
    debriding plexal trees—

Have you ever plighted your troth, & broken it?
    Have you eaten with such greed that you cast it

up again? Upgraded, daylight
    is once again saved. It worships me

like a knife these evenings—promoted
    despite the still-cheap, bare impairment

of thickets, woods, the civet, fasting
    garderobe at all margins.

I prefer the Apostle's counsel—
    "use a little wine for thy stomach's sake,"

& stare it down: dyspeptic gleam.
    Are you wont to ride through grain

when you could go to one side?
    With splintered boldness

bloom invades the fields, against whose bare shanks
    I muster, join ranks.

Two Shrifts

In defrocked yonder of waning winter,
cerise pasture flanks, deer thin & ruminant,

don't mistake me for an enameled cartouche
of wet light hung beyond porch columns,

& the mistletoe-infested oak a tilted scale
etched there, swallows in sinuous ambit.

If I'd written "in amorous flight" I might
have betrayed myself, how much I still wish

to always bear if not wear
the shift of your gaze upon me.

*

White-knuckled, soprano, high
was I among inchoate film

budding the trees we topped, bent
against a railing, the growled fruit

of your throat, passional, at my nape.
Contracted as pilgrims, we were

parousial emblems of the air that,
miraculously scarred with our gasped names,

27

held us—I couldn't say *where*—
in mind? at hand?

On a cloud descending or, conversely,
while being lifted up?

Those bodies we were before
we climbed gazed up deeply into us,

glass messages extravenous,
in mortal transfusion of flesh & gust.

Cathartes aura

With human succor, this caped guild
tugs, scouring a struck doe,

padding, pecking, sidestepping the thrown flank
on soft, useless feet, one in pose horaltic,

wings spread as though for privacy,
horrible striated legs streaked with urine,

cooling them at their heated toil,
carcass, tar, windshield glare, scrotal necks

& bald pink pates adapted for such recessed,
messy work. Masters of this task,

yet unconscious of any wish to help,
to partake in the dimension that makes one

transform. My hair's on end,
watching them resettle in the rear-view.

What's heavy must seem light,
what light, heavy. I know this,

in the lapse under which one staggers,
carrying things, even when the itinerary

has suffered, with equal care,
fragment & flight, the artisanal laws.

St. Brontë

When does one's beloved become a concept?
Maître, I wrote. Intelligence continues

despite a headache. Seed thrown
from the stoop to birds, winged hunger.

I am unable. To not—.
I am in want. Thank you for not

sending facts. Which would break me,
jealousy with its sister exotica.

Here: morning milk, its mortification.
The kitchen's a stable.

Rooms bloom inside me I can't enter.
At least not specifically.

The failing is mine, no doubt.
To abstract is to surrender.

St. Hope. St. Story. Is syntax erotic?
If so, please. Please read. Here.

Bone Orchard Lunch Hour

Tomorrow rhymes with sorrow
as a co-ed on a cell phone crosses the cemetery,

sighing *that's so not on my vagenda!*
& this old haunt seems less and less a sidebar

hunched ghetto, stone torsos scabbed
by storms, mossed epaulets, names drab

beneath bird-lime badges, & more a beveled runway,
troubling the hydrangea, cerulean cedar dragée,

me, as billiards of black walnuts kiss,
already fallen, each a fabulous promise

of shade, future feasts, dank hulls
of cerebral grub pressing into the skull-

&-joint garden regardless of the perfumed
girl already a blasted text beyond these rooms.

God's Gym

In blunder of dusk I negotiate rush hour
past the strip-mall fitness center,

plate glass tableaux of bodies in treadmill
silhouette, an elbow in the signage above gone dark.

I can hear from here the earbuds stair-stepping,
bottomless techno sham, no bridge, no left hand,

& consider the fit of cherry blossoms
that blew against my blouse this morning.

You sent them to me;
also the cursive plum branch in ghostly waver,

blue jay already swallowed by white sky. Lover,
I could say, or little brother, consider the Shakers,

their simple holes and pegs complicated by glossolalia
of twitch and stomp *as if you had a thousand years*

to live, and their celibate shafts of conversion,
as if you were to die tomorrow

of adoption, the upper room of the heart emptying
into tongues of esophageal fire.

Spring Fever

Of course these lavender & cream leaflets,
the dogwood's infant handbills—

exquisite & vulnerable as the triangular
flap of a heart's valve—would open

tonight, timed to hurt that small, shamed part
of me, secretly, zealously sad

& prone to black stockings
in the rival gloam of coupling,

of fair copies fingering tapas in the mirrored,
olivewood smoke of bed & breakfast anniversaries.

If only I could feel italicized by all this complication.
Instead I feel my name lost in the typo

cry of a lone, silly goose flying south
despite a pornographically pink bustier of blooms.

The Irises

for Charles Wright

A fly quizzical among tufted causeways,
blue sudden avenues spumed overnight from spears.

O silk, my throat closing around a sob.
That fly again, minute leaden tank, thread-hooves,

busy, busy, to whom I mean nothing.
Relief in this. Yet to me he's singing beside the dugout, the ditch,

cosmic with pathologies. A grave matter,
that perfume—father, mother, son, & daughter—

those phrases—no hands, no feet, how else depart,
eyes opened without ceasing—

why I can't disturb their bruised hymning,
why I gather them all inside, until I'll know—

Kismet

Our limbs in such
          ligature
that, world adjourned,
would even God have recognized

us as human?
          A swallowing.
Then pearling scree at the sill
of—where?—me

or a tree shivering
          with wings?
O light jacket of the air!
I know your hand was—there—

a place impossible, else,
          to open
to the light
& survive. Years

this way,
          sun drifting by
on a raft of shadow.
Un-asylumed breathing.

What doesn't love
          restraint?
I felt divinity pour itself
into your body's icon—& live.

Black Snake

Does this longest day define me,
sleepless as I always am with solstice qualms,

white, extreme stagger of light refusing
to depart bamboo, amethyst contusion, the yard

across which I drag a garden hose?
From an open upper-story window

a recording of that ululating indie harpist girl,
my daughter's new favorite singer, shrieks

in faux child-voice of harts and velvet
prisons. I want to like her music,

but instead it makes me want to gnaw rocks.
Apricot pendulum lyre ticking

in the locust, blue fieldstones
of the crumbling fence, old crush

on the world whose beauty I've always feared
to see directly—will that leave me, too,

despite years that never brought me the weightless
grace I thought I'd become for myself, or anyone?

I hope not, bending to the spigot
that suddenly moves, uncoils, all my years

rushing like ebony water around a pier
then bellying off into the dark, wanting nothing.

Friday Motet

Day ends, chainlinks the subdivision,
its unspeakable splay

vying with shiver from stadium lights
igniting the high-school soccer fields,

stropping the rooftops & bird-bridled bamboo
with a cleansing flame. *Eleven, twelve,*

fourteen, twenty!, a boy cries, uncovering his eyes
in the fields, and from here: dusk, scrambling,

shrieks in broom sedge, the gasp
of their fathers' beer cans opening in porch shadows,

one of them saying, *Man, she fucked. . .*
she something me. . . something, something. . . ,

sense lost as I mouth evening prayer—
"you who are worthy at all times to be praised

by happy voices"—into the opened window.
Last night, my friend dreamed of his death,

a tumor in his mouth, under the tongue he used
to speak into the receiver, telling me

"This is my last poem." When we end,
will it be as when, for private reasons,

we live gloriously in one another
for an hour, more, as long as we are given

—not criminal, but moored, like these vines—
kudzu, honeysuckle, belts unfleshed

& undeniable with incensed horizon,
a reason to bear lying down apart?

Hang Fire

Get drunk and call it Paris
—Paul Celan

Splotchy, sudden rashers of rain
swipe all afternoon the concrete terrain

of the amphitheater; then fickle eruptions
of sun sparkle the dripping hustings,

the green tiltyard of wilting umbrellas.
Summer's sprawl encroaches, threatening

to unedge even what would always,
like a heroine in James, delay—not say—

withdraw—exactly as every border now somersaults,
rampant, its brickwork strictures, shawls

of luxuriant dominant mold, smoke & bier
bingeing on air, bidding *love this way*, without fear.

After Hokusai

For years, raw data. Pigment!
    Tung oil, fishscales, deer skin, pearls.
The feats, the rush, the brush,

performances insatiable: at 44,
    on the outskirts of Edo,
paint flooding a saké cask, hoisting a reed broom

across an ocean of composite paper
    600 feet long, gawkers
from the temple roof shouting *Daruma!*,

Daruma!, drawn Buddha whose mouth
    a horse could amble through,
eyes the size of men; still more years spent

showing off—indigo fingers, hen eggs scarlet,
    bamboo stick-ends,
sketches executed upside-down,

antic at the house of a shōgun,
    pitching across a courtyard scroll
a furl of Prussian blue,

then chasing a cock, its fisted feet
    dipped in vermillion,
across that tributary, boasting afterwards,

"Maple-leaves on the Tatsua River!"—
        then, climacteric, urn-thick cocks
tinted purple, in small, soft-bound limited editions,

lovers cramped into the pages, four tight corners,
        labial folds, shell pale
kimonos, octopi prongs forcing mouths

& mons prone in sea-foam—.
        But for this late self-portrait,
seamed neck, torso crooked over

bent cane: mere bone-black ink, sumi,
        & just a ghostly, pulse-point pentimenti
of cinnabar, the soul

pushing its way out, regret,
        what Older Wife once saw:
rust stains at my robe's cinch,

estrus of Younger Wife.
        No point in saying a blade,
my hand, knife, at the pear wood block.

Her hurt showed me color:
        brief shame, ego seeping away
into blanched, untranslatable sky.

Graven

Amidst doubt's claustral, nada stylings—
broken bathroom fan, crotch the traveling headlamps fling—

this pursed, worried pansy, the godless clock.
Forget that. To imagine what's unreal (soul, the Other, desire, blah)

in a hook-hung, emptied robe carcass, or curtains lax & gray,
is not my passion. Instead to say

what's all too real in terms of what's beyond
existence!—perhaps impossible here, in words,

to tell. Still, try: inkling flare, japonica flooded & skeletal.
The dawn genitive, hived, unstoppable.

St. Vogue

With a route in *voguer*, to sail—
    as *longing* is root to Lent—
so the glamour of failing is again in season,

Gothic vanes—cocks, ships—
    in a bully wind.
Junket, sortie, sashay, leaves

too on the runaway, umbrella bones,
    as cold reminds the soul,
unplunderable word, to awake,

preside. But where? Harvested cuffs
    & pelts of fur?
The signature bag, vellum abyss?

Or in this harem cobweb that captures
    the face before the swipe, the tear,
the alas already outmoded away?

"*I have drunk, and seen the spider*"
from *The Winter's Tale*

That unrequited late-season blur
in the pippins, slurring the glans

of Russian sage with yellow-jackets,
was trumped by your arm, its filigree of fur,

nap I've stroked with my tongue,
altering time by motion in a world

that somehow made us possible.
It blenched the lawn, your halo

of columns, oak-leaf hydrangea; *I'm just,*
you said, *holding up a mirror,*

invisible frame fingered as by quotation marks,
lifted from your lap after our talk of why

this home, why not another, why stay,
why not? and despite the leafing shirr

of heat, a bare-branch call
of star-tramped abstinence lit my bones.

I looked through it, into your face.
Dare I speak of what I saw?

Any held breath is wish for something
to happen. In what did not, I think

I see your meaning. To abandon
a dream, a hope? No. But rather know a force

that seethes into your heart,
not mine, but mine.

Dead Moth

In every lonely place,
    an altar,

gulf between adjective
    & noun, uncurling,

pale green in stiff thumbnail
    sarcophagus, mica sheen.

Time wasted, & worse, looms,
    as a bit of the reverend

dark road, why say very right,
    breaks off, upheaves,

unfolding despite last light,
    despite light.

St. Home

Upon Penelope, most worn in love and thought,
Athena cast a glance like a gray sea
Lifting her.
  from *The Odyssey*

Hard frost drops, buckles black blooms
in pewter gleam. I am loom.

What to weave? Silver threads of my head,
the dog's cinnamon fur. Barbed stems,

the spider's nocturnal script?
Hair that is both plant & animal

as day expires fast, as if to obliterate
the distinction. Separations are never clear.

The lone twist of pure rose-flesh among the canes;
impress of the deer's cleft hoof, vaginal there.

It was warm when he sailed away.
Reunion is not illusion, these boots of leaves

whisper. Rime shackles my ankles
as promise dons time's veil.

Hibernalphilia

Triangular glasses, brumal volts, gin,
frescade of pearls, plucked, sunned olives,

grave albino onions, juniper nip & the cusp of snow,
we sip slow, as at a glacier's lip. Holy day.

I'm thinking fingerbone salad, the marginalia
of Emily Brontë, intricate skeleton keys,

not blade but the pierced heart, the bow
to which torque must be applied.

That blue note of exile in your eyes.
Meeting mine you say *The way you inhale*

semen oysters rosewater ordure of armpit, footsole,
I smell time. I meaning you. You smell time.

Alone along the Interstate, later, runnels rapt into ice,
sun sinks, aguish, an amber smut, ruttish

behind black roofs, crotched ridge.
Why miss any chance to be changed?

I'm ready, you said, back in our niveous cups,
gelid narcotic by which I mentally undressed you.

You called my drink *chaste*. The intoxication
love brings when we mean to gladden,

mouths boreal and high. Terrified, beautiful.
Unashamed. They are the same.

You, For Now

Sacred is the solar year, heavenly coins moving fixedly:
vise closing, the migrations. Sickle, gnashing moon.

Where is my purse? is her refrain from dementia's
unsprung love seat, fetish stand-in for her stolen head.

Especially at this X-hatched signature
devolvement of the staircase, what could be

more complicated? a crone on hands & knees
on unlit treads, fugitive as her husband sleeps—

the room she'll reach—as elsewhere minds
that might well be original sing with bodies locked

in regnant testament—*you, you, you know
who I am*—even as the galaxy changes shifts,

& one must clock in, the other walk to the parking lot, an oak leaf
sliding its flattened petition against the pewter curb,

past a boy proffering pamphlets no one will take,
while she's in the dark on a floor, no one she can name.

Iconoclast

This evening, as though I'd slept
a thousand yearnings, beaks open again in the yellow willow
      the lost song of belong,

cardinals silverly chipping saucers
as petals, blue with dusk, spot the drive.
      That stranger this morning,

weeping in her passing car.
Mute, behind glass, the future again,
      slam of two or more situations coming apart.

Still, to know you in this hormonal
endgame, scarlet stand of shivering maples,
      is to live twice.

Dusk Binge

Don't go, luxe archipelago
flush with swallows,

indigo island clouds,
raw, dank carousal

of privet hedge, bamboo.
Stars analect & blue.

Isn't that Divinity Somebody, back-lit
by your gilded draught,

dream I'll hold all night
in argument, sleight

against your goading,
skull as ash, unlit window?

On knees stained by the zodiac
I hold nothing back;

self in augend now, low tide—
a sky increased by subside—

After the Meeting, a Red Fox

If ever more ravened, junked, numb-sconced
I could not recall it, sopping in aftermath

dusk's blossom bock, ink-musk ale
at rusted window screen, the annual carnival

a neon embolism blurring the horizon's black seam
that from the brine of my dispirits

struck me as the portajohn & ticket-littered
portal of hypocrisy and the soul's mojo shutting down.

Then you, scrabble in the bamboo,
fluent rapacious pelt, burnt, elegant-booted streak

flecking the despond no longer just mine
with a shiver estival that—even as language cages

it now, a loping scriptural and starving—
every word of it I winged to you then a barbarous traveling.

St. Bed of Snow

Would rather be lying there? No.
Though my pillow is a backwards-wound watch.

Cream linen of another country
where I lay in troth, hands pressed

to the wall, those pages. . . .
Tonight, opium protocols of a full moon

blanch alluvial oak leaves.
Rather lie sheeted in frost there & pray

for the forgiveness of you,
absent friend? Yes. Yes. Words

failed me. O swallow them
back. Rackety wind muslins the beeches,

illusion of a calendar in storm.
Autumn to winter. Turn again. Don't end.

Watch

Time, carnal cradle,
do we sleep in the feminine?

If so, why instead this casket
of sexless moonlight,

second hands gathering drams
of unspoken words,

the window's ladder of shadow?
Interior of the letter "O,"

tick of a starving dialect,
latch the bomb makes, nursing oblivion:

I am out-waiting them.
Pen scratch, carcass stalking

the dipthong hours of near-dawn,
is this suffering? I know

these instants until you arrive
as my rivals. Defeat them with your coming.

Outliving Emily

When it is May, if May return.
—Emily Dickinson
(10 December 1830–15 May 1886)

Knobby corms buried
above the buried dog. Three.
One for each child grown and gone away.

"This is freedom!" you mimed with a key in air.
And bulb noses poked emerald through secret black leaves
last March. Asphyxiation. Horrible dragging

of breath in and out before the chaired watchers,
all privacy choked. Early April: Poet's Narcissus
above the dog's grave. Don't touch.

May advanced. Austin's diary: "would not wake again
this side. The day was awful."
Summer stormed in, wild goddess,

stone wall toppled, shingles stripped off,
electric stakes plunging. But rain
brought the day-lilies for which you were "Lunatic."

My mother, crone in unmatched shoes
on the wrong feet, cut a divot through the forehead
of her paper doll. Ulysses S. Grant.

My father and I canned tomatoes, ten bushels.
Seeds in my hair and clothes for days. Fortnight later,
long bridge back from a week at the beach,

I can't stop crying. Your Norcross, one of few
from whom you did not run, had traveled away.
Hours, weeks, the futile saving of daylight.

"Homeless at home," you wrote. And yet.
And yet, *to disappear enhances*—
Peeper canticles. Crickets. The last mourning rags

dangle on the rosehips. Cinnamon bits.
Frosted fence. Then winter,
brutal, voweled, but returning light,

bringing my gypsy, despair
dispelled. This year my blade's
a yes among the stems. A new dog pulls

back outside. Moon-globe streetlamps
make cul-de-sacs exotic. Insects ignite my leash arm,
fly. Abide. Unadjourned. And you ever by.

Is There a Magic Word?

Held breath is blue.
    So too, as to train-tracks
with leather straps & villainous velvet,

a flocked nineteenth-century album
    erupts into danger: our Heroine
to desk & chair legs bound.

Dear Reader, one wonder
    speaks of another.
So she is page, & the author

therefore wraps
    also her neck with a chain
of keys, clocks—

but not yet. First the gripped
    wrists. He is above
with his—blue—swept here, & silken there.

Blinding tides & a wish to tongue
    green oils, sediment,
scarlet peppercorns;

blue soles now flush her heart.
    White panic, ribs
corseting blue, the world gone

to fires mawing timber, gambrel,
    the ash of it blizzarding,
filming eyes, throat

with a question she would ask
    if she could only,
hail burning every place

he's yet to rescue.
    As he bends, spank-red seam
of the split blue-fish,

chandelier crown crashing
    toward violence
of the pelvic floor.

But still not yet. Steel
    understudy of rails heat, singe.
Gnashing, Biting air.

A guest, she is in theory
    still alive. A wet ribboning.
Where is this leading

them, hand to her mouth
    when it floods her,
lock parting into him.

St. Tulip

Flamed bandana skulls,
stems tight in elastic bundle.

But over days, shiva-limbed,
sucking up water, they elongate,

ambrosial pneumatics. Mercurial.
Tabletop flesh-tap.

Do we ever really leave the body,
lonely gods, even for you?

Leave ourselves, maybe,
sleeves of black stockings,

holes of sweated camisole,
as coral rafts of quince

& blue strappy shadows
imply what, a soul?

O other world, eat me out.
Seasonless, because of you.

Music Lessons

For so long, these exercises,
    clots of grapes hung from pergola staves,

red fox arpeggio, shiver of cedar, *abandon, abandon,*
    moths threshing the window-screen.

So why weep into the keyboard of dimming field,
    ensnared, wired for loss, one note still to sound

between this day's scale & its erasure?
    What does it matter now, that wedging of wood shims

between gripe-clad fingers all night to extend one's range
    one, two, notes beyond the octave?

Afraid was what I didn't want to be,
    turning the last page. Now I see

there is no landing, just the last tread & rise,
    then the crypt of stars.

Before that, for as long as possible,
    the exquisite, felted climb & fall.